SUCCESS IS IN YOUR HANDS

Pocket Size Quotes

The potential for Wealth
is guided by your Everyday Thoughts

Inspirational Thoughts of How to Attract WEALTH

Jonathan Edison, M.Ed.
Author of *How I Became a Millionaire at 30!*

J E E Publishing

JUN - - 2005

This book is dedicated to
my father, Larry E. Edison

for his courage and unceasing commitment
to excellence, his family and God.

*Dad, you are a true Warrior and Trailblazer in history.
I'm proud to be your son and
I thank God for your life.*

*Your Son,
Jonathan E. Edison
"The Prince of Possibilities"*

Table of Contents

❧

ANYTHING IS POSSIBLE

It works if you work it!

— Dr. Johnnie Coleman

The moment that you try, you've won half the battle.

—JE

It's amazing what you can accomplish
when you don't know you can't do it

— ANON

*I didn't know I couldn't swim until I was done
swimming.*

—JE

What we see in life depends mainly upon what we look for.

— JOHN LUBBOCK

When I wake up in the morning, I truly believe I'm on a mission to find wealth, happiness and peace.

— JE

What you think means more than anything else in your life

— GEORGE MATTHEW ADAMS

If you think you can, you will.

—JE

You can have anything you want in life if
you want it desperately enough. You must
want it with an inner exuberance that
erupts through the skin and joins the
energy that created the world.

— SHELIAH GRAHAM

*Go after everything that you want in life
as if your life depended on it. Why? Because it
does.*

—JE

85% of people believe what they see and
the other 15% believe what they hear.
That's why I have my name on both of my
private jets.

— WILLIE E. GARY

Don't be afraid to show God off.
He provided the blessing so rub it
in the devil's face.

—JE

You don't get in life what you deserve;
You get in life what you can negotiate.

— La-Van Hawkins

Stop crying and make something happen for yourself. Don't let your genius go to waste.

—JE

Possibility blindness is a disease
that we cannot afford to take hold of.

— LES BROWN

*The possibility for you to succeed is greater for
you than to fail.*

— JE

Greatness is the capacity to go from failure
to failure without losing enthusiasm.

— WINSTON CHURCHILL

*If you want to experience greatness, be
prepared to take a few bruises.*

—JE

Whenever you are asked if you can do a
job, tell 'em "Certainly I can!" Then get
busy and find out how to do it.

— THEODORE ROOSEVELT

*Fake it until you can make it. Use your talent
reservoir to draw from
when you have to do the impossible.*

—JE

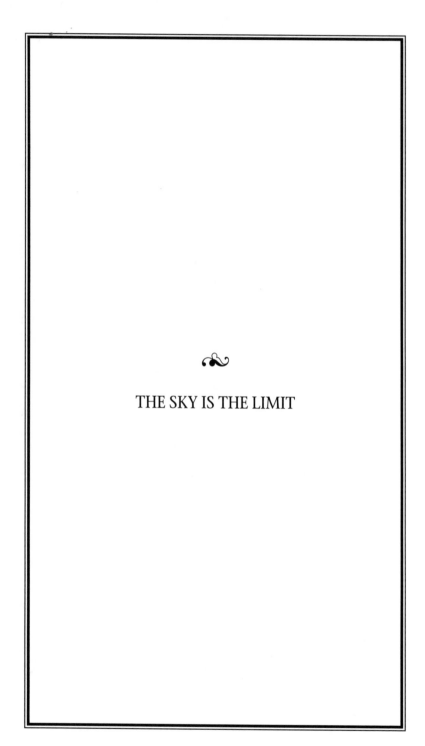

THE SKY IS THE LIMIT

The sky is the limit; you just keep on pressing on and you can have what you want and be what you want.

— Notorious B.I.G.

I firmly believe that every individual on the planet can achieve greatness if they have the willingness to commit.

—JE

When the Dream is big enough, the odds
do matter.

— DEXTER YAEGER

Think about the reward, not the challenge.

— JE

If you decide to develop what you do well
and master yourself,
your determination and gifts will take you
places that will amaze you.

— LES BROWN

*Practice, practice, practice your craft
and the only outcome can be success.*

—JE

The greatest mistake a man can make is to
be afraid to make one.

— ELBERT HUBBARD

Be prepared to fail on your quest for greatness.

—*JE*

Grab a chance and you won't be sorry
for a might-have-been moment.

— ARTHUR RANSOM

*Everything that you set your mind to can be
accomplished if you are willing to take the first
step, which is commitment.*

—JE

Only those who dare to fail greatly can ever
achieve greatness.

— Robert F. Kennedy

*Failure is a teaching tool that can be used to
craft out excellence.*

— JE

Believe in the best, think your best, study your best, never be satisfied with less than your best, try your best, and in the long run things with turn out for the best.

— ANON

The mind is the battleground for infinite success.

—JE

To Abraham — I will give you all your eyes
can see.

— SCRIPTURE

What ever you want out of life,
you can have it if you can conceptualize it in
your mind's eye.

—JE

If you want to soar like an eagle,
you have to leave those pigeons alone.

— RAY JOHNSON

*Keep negative, big mouth, non-producing
people out of your life.*

— JE

Let not young souls be smothered out
before they do quaint deeds
and fully flaunt their pride.

— RACHEL LINDSAY

*Don't hold on to your gifts. Use them, share
them, cultivate them
before your time runs out.*

— JE

MILLIONS FOR YOUR THOUGHTS

Every big dream begins with a small idea.

— Thomas Edison

Think Big, Live Big, Give Big.

—JE

I wonder what blessings are looking for me today?

— DR. LEROY THOMPSON

Adjust your thinking to believe that someone is looking to bless you everyday of your life.

— JE

There is not enough darkness in the world
to extinguish the light of one small candle.

— SPANISH PROVERB

*You become the majority once you stand up to
be heard.*

—JE

Without leaps of imagination, or dreaming, we lose the excitement of possibilities. Dreaming, after all, is a form of planning.

— GLORIA STEINEM

Your dream of greatness is an extreme possibility if planned properly.

—JE

Be not conformed to this world; renew
your mind daily.

— SCRIPTURE

*Do what YOU have to do to make things
happen for YOU.*

—JE

I thought about it so I did it.

— WALT DISNEY

Think about yourself accomplishing great things and you will.

— JE

Immense power is acquired by assuring
yourself in your secret reveries that you
were born to control affairs.

— ANDREW CARNEGIE

Validate and qualify yourself.
Don't always look for others to do it for you.

—*JE*

If you expect nothing, you're apt to be
surprised. You'll get it.

— MALCOLM FORBES

*Your expectation level controls your level of
receiving.*

—JE

I truly believe in the power of positivity
and how it affects your life.

— OPRAH WINFREY

*The more positive you are, the more you make
yourself available to be blessed.*

— JE

Once I'm in the zone,
there is no stopping me!

— MICHAEL JORDAN

*When a forest fire starts, it's virtually
impossible to put it out.*

— JE

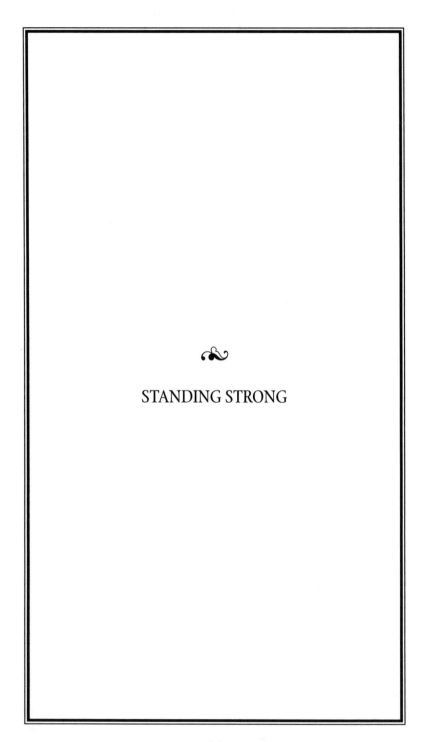

STANDING STRONG

We are all struggling with something,
but it is how we handle it is what matters.

— TERRIE WILLIAMS

Don't wimp out. Get your chin off your chest,
get your shoulders back
and stand up and be a man.

—JE

If I lose, I'll walk away and never feel bad ...
Because I did all I could, there was nothing
more to do.

— JOE FRAZIER

Losing is nothing. Just don't quit!

— JE

Yeah, I'm locked up right now,
but I still have the number 1 album
in the country.

— 2 PAC SHAKUR

*You may be in a difficult situation
but you still have Greatness within you.*

—JE

They said I would never make it, I was too young, immature and I lacked leadership. Now I'm the youngest NBA player in history to hold three championship rings.

— KOBE BRYANT

If you listen to negative people, you will never fulfill the destiny that God has planned for your life.

— JE

When life knocks you down, make sure
you fall on your back,
because if you can look up, you can get up.

— LES BROWN

*A major part of paying your dues is taking a
few lumps upside the head.*

— JE

If there is no struggle, there is no progress.
Those who profess to favor freedom and
yet deprecate agitation are men who want
crops without plowing up the ground.
They want rain without thunder and
lightning. They want the ocean without the
awful roar of its many waters.

— U.S. STATESMAN
FREDERICK DOUGLAS

*Stop saying that you want greatness, wealth,
respect and affluence if you are too damn lazy
to go after it!*

—JE

Adversity is part of the damn job!

— COLEMAN A. YOUNG

Expect negative things and negative people to surface once you make the commitment to your dream.

— JE

I just thank God for the life that he contin-
ues to breath in me.

— RICHARD PRYOR

*In all things, give God thanks for His goodness
and mercy.*

— JE

Try being young, black and wealthy.

— SEAN "PUFF DADDY" COMBS

Be careful of what you ask for.
You just might get it.

—*JE*

Freeing slaves is my only concern.
"Are you the ONE?"

— HARRIET TUBMAN

It doesn't matter what's going on around you;
stay focused and carry out your God-
appointed mission.

—JE

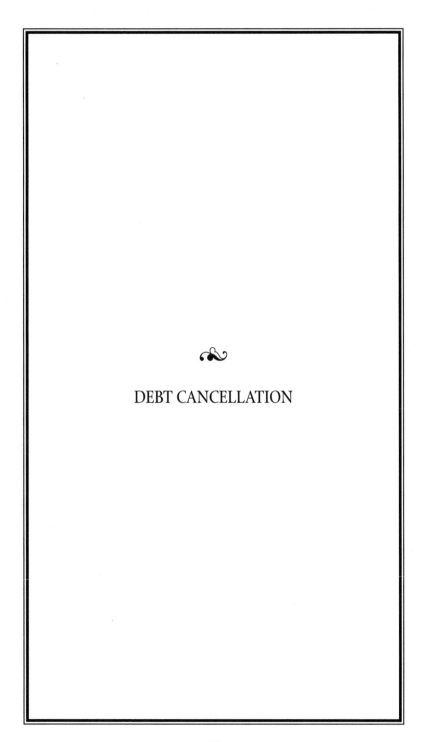

DEBT CANCELLATION

Money cometh to me now!

— Dr. Leroy Thompson

Command money to obey you with the words
of your mouth.

— JE

Money is a tool that can be used to change the world.

— Dr. Crefflo A. Dollar

Don't love money; allow money to spread love.

— *JE*

Wealth is in the hand of the believer.

— ANON

If you truly believe that you are supposed to be wealthy, you will.

— JE

I control money;
money doesn't control me.

— BOB JOHNSON

Money is extremely seductive,
so be careful as you handle it.

—JE

I knew I was destined to be rich even living
in the projects.

— MASTER P. "PERCY MILLER"

Wealth begins with an inner feeling of it.

—JE

The minute you change your thinking, you
can change your bank account as well.

— BISHOP T.D. JAKES

*Don't wrestle with the fact that you are
supposed to be rich.*

—JE

Weeds choke out your seeds, so get the
weeds out of your life.

— BISHOP KEITH A. BUTLER

Negative people, thoughts, habits and beliefs
will keep you from your place of wealth.

—JE

I am the master of money and it follows
me everywhere that I go.

— ANON

Money is always in circulation —
so tap into it

— JE

I'm out of debt and all of my needs
are met.

— ANON

If you believe in total freedom,
the first stage is being debt free.

—JE

Owe no man anything, but to love one another: for he that loveth another hath fulfilled the law.

— ROMANS 13:8

Stop running up your credits cards and live a debt free life.

— JE

NO RISK, NO REWARD

Many people miss out on opportunity
because it is dressed up
in overalls and it looks like work.

— THOMAS EDISON

If you're a lazy individual, you will never have
an opportunity in life
to achieve anything.

—JE

You may be disappointed if you fail, but
doomed if you don't try.

— BEVERLY SILLS

*Get out of your comfort zone and try
something new for a change.*

— JE

It's never to late to become what you might have been.

— GEORGE ELIOT

I don't care what your age is — if you have breath, you qualify for Greatness.

— JE

We have not because we ask not.

— SCRIPTURE

If you ask people for help to achieve your dreams, help will come.

— JE

You will become as small as your
controlling desire, as great as your
dominant aspiration, so don't be afraid to
take the plunge.

— A<small>NON</small>

Stop talking about it and be about it!

—JE

Good things come to those who wait, but
they are the things left over by the people
who hustle.

— ABRAHAM LINCOLN

*Don't cry if you miss out because
you were asleep.*

—JE

Most of us go through life holding back
when we know deep down inside that
we've got more work to do.

— ANON

*Even if you have achieved some level of success,
don't be content.*

—JE

If you're not willing to risk, you're not willing to grow. If you're not willing to grow, you're not willing to be happy. And if you're not willing to be happy, then what else is there?

— LES BROWN

If you want all the things that you desire to materialize, you have to put forth a maximum effort.

— JE

One never finds anything perfectly pure
and ... exempt from danger.

— Niccolo Machiavelli

Stop looking for the easy way out all the time.

—JE

All life is chance. So take it! The person
who goes furthest is the one who is willing
to do and dare.

— DALE CARNEGIE

*If you don't take a chance on yourself,
you're cheating yourself out of life.*

—JE

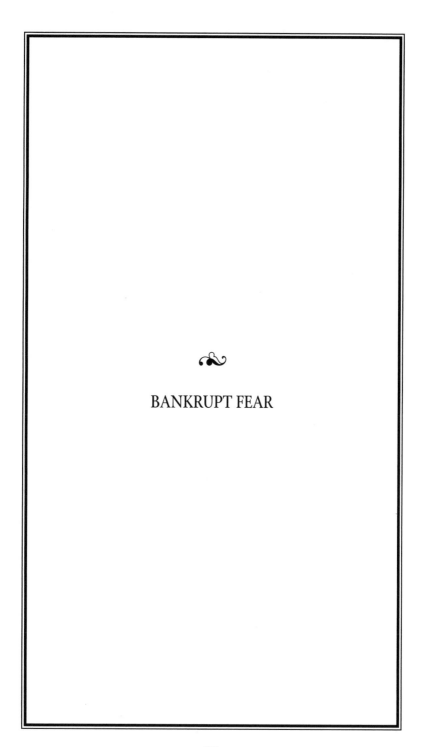

BANKRUPT FEAR

Fear is only what you make it; it has no
special power.

— ANON

*A shadow on the sidewalk can't hurt you.
I promise.*

—JE

Did you know that fear is actually afraid?

— Dr. Crefflo A. Dollar

Action will cure fear.

—*JE*

All men are afraid in battle. The coward is
the one who lets his fear overcome
his sense of duty. Duty is the essence of
manhood.

— GENERAL GEORGE S. PATTON

*It's OK to be afraid but just don't allow it to
overcome you.*

—JE

Feel the fear and do it anyway.

— ANON

Fear is natural and so is success,
once you master it.

—JE

There's nothing I'm afraid of like
scared people.

— ROBERT FROST

*Stay away from people who use fear as a
crutch.*

—JE

The only thing that we have to fear is fear itself — nameless, unreasoning, unjustified terror, which paralyzes needed efforts to convert retreat into advance.

— Franklin Delano Roosevelt

If you accept the fact that fear is inevitable,
you will be able to use it
as a springboard into greatness.

— JE

I don't think of myself as a poor, deprived
ghetto girl who made good. I think of
myself as somebody who from an early age
knew I was responsible for myself,
and I had to make good.

— OPRAH WINFREY

*The fear of negativity can also cause you to be
successful.*

—JE

There's much to be said for challenging
fate instead of ducking behind it.

— DIANE TRILLING

*Take life head on; don't allow it to
intimidate you.*

—JE

I wish somebody would tell me no!

— Cloraine M. Turner
(my Granny)

In order to be successful, you have to develop a "no matter what" attitude.

—JE

God has not given us the spirit of fear,
but of a strong mind and power.

— SCRIPTURE

*God is responsible for your greatness, gifts and
talents — not FEAR.*

—JE

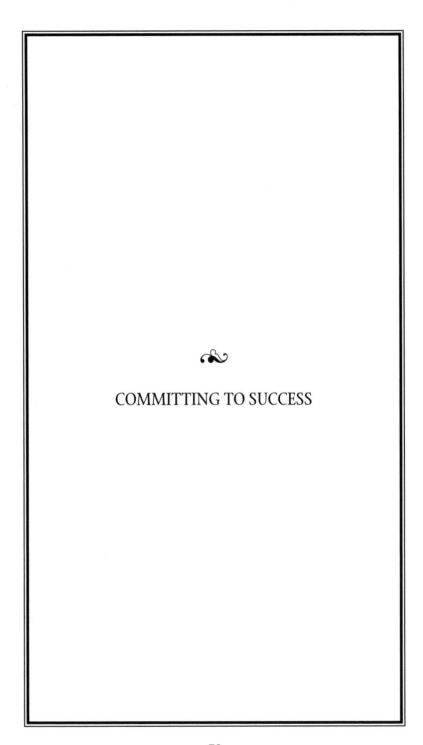

COMMITTING TO SUCCESS

Success is out there; all you have to do is
go and get it.

—J.C. PENNEY

*If you look for success, I guarantee you will
find it.*

—JE

Once you make the commitment, then
providence moves too,
which is all the gifts of God working on
your behalf.

— ANON

*Get started and God has an obligation
to help you.*

— JE

Prove me now and I will pour you out a blessing and you won't have room enough to receive it.

— SCRIPTURE

God is waiting on you — you're not waiting on Him.

— JE

You must be willing to do the things that
others won't do today to have things
tomorrow that others won't have.

— ANON

*If you prepare, plan, and carry out your
mission while others are asleep, expect to be
resting while others are working.*

—JE

Once you get going, it's hard to stop.
— BILL GATES

Live your life to the fullest.
— JE

Do it once to demonstrate or prove that you can do it. Do it again to see if you like it. Then do it a third time to see if whether or not you want to keep on doing it.

— ELEANOR ROOSEVELT

Find out if you love what you do because if you don't love it, it will always seem like work.

—JE

Let the dead bury the dead; come down
and follow me.

— JESUS

Get excited and be happy about life.

— JE

Inspiration is easy — implementation is
the hard part.

— BOB TAYLOR

*Just don't read books. Take the information
and put it to use.*

— JE

You don't get in life what you want —
you get in life what you are.

— Anon

*In the long run, what you give to life is what
you get from life.*

— JE

Vacillating people seldom succeed. They
seldom win the solid respect of their
fellows. Successful men and women are
very careful in reaching decisions, and very
persistent and determined in action
thereafter.

— L.G. ELLIOT

*Persistence is one of the master keys to unlock
the door to a more fulfilled life.*

— JE

COUNT YOUR BLESSINGS

I thank the Lord for blessings big and
small; for spring's warm glow and
songbird's welcome call; for autumn's hue
and winter's white snow shawl. I thank
Thee for the harvest rich with grain; for all
trees and the quiet shadowed lane ...
but most of all I thank Thee for Thy Love.

— RALPH GAITHER
(written while a POW
in North Vietnam)

*Take a look around and realize the
magnificence of God.*

—JE

Life may be hard, but it is also wonderful.

— ANON

Regardless of the tough times in life, always remember the good.

— JE

The mere sense of living is joy enough.

— EMILY DICKINSON

Without life, what else is there?

—JE

I live therefore I am.

— ANON

As long as I have breath in my body,
I will commit to living my life to the fullest.

—JE

There's nothing sweeter than life itself.

— DON KING

How can one deny the joy and pleasure that
God provides us all?

— JE

Health is a blessing that money
cannot buy.

— ANON

Without good health, money is useless.

—JE

Think of the ills of which you are exempt.

— JOSEPH JOUBERT

If you're not sick, thank God for your health.

— JE

Thank God every morning that you get up;
that you have something to do that needs
to be done.

— BISHOP KEITH A. BUTLER

*Be careful not to complain because the
universe is listening.*

— JE

Life is not guaranteed a sure thing.

— ANON

You only have one life to live so give it your all.

—JE

The best things are nearest: breath in your
nostrils, light in your eyes,
flowers at your feet, duties at your hand,
the path of God just before you.
Then do not grasp at the stars, but do life's
plain common work as it comes,
certain that daily duties and daily bread
are the sweetest things in life.

— ROBERT LOUIS STEVENSON

*Take a deep breath and feel God's goodness
fill your lungs.*

—JE

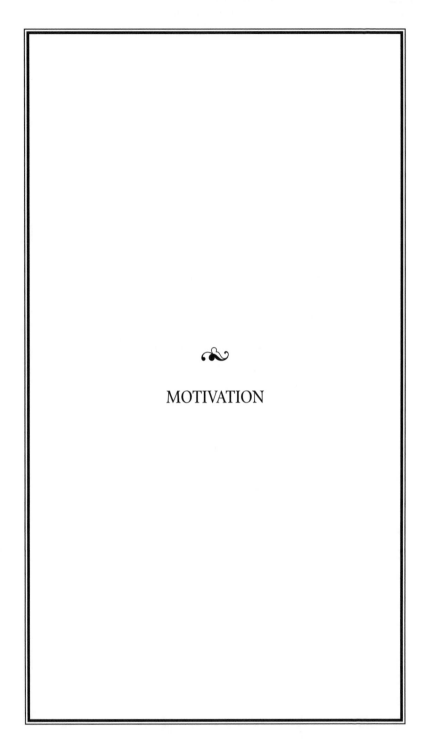

MOTIVATION

The fact that I'm breathing motivates me
to make music.

— DMX — Earl Simmons

Motivation begins with appreciation.

—JE

Why ask why; just do.

— ANON

*Stop questioning your ability and
take the plunge.*

— JE

If you don't like something, change it.
If you can't change it, change your attitude.

— MAYA ANGELOU

Attitude dictates altitude.

—JE

You don't control tomorrow, so you better
do it today.

— ANON

*Don't procrastinate on your Millionaire idea
— get started on it today!*

— JE

If you keep on doing what you're doing,
you will keep on getting what you're
getting.

— STEPHEN COVEY

*Insanity is doing something over and over
and expecting a different result.*

—JE

Many people die at age 21 and don't get
buried until they are 65.

— LES BROWN

*Don't stop living and find yourself
waiting to die.*

— JE

I firmly believe that in a man's finest hour
— his greatest fulfillment
to all he holds dear — is that moment
when he has worked his heart out for a
good cause and lies exhausted on the field
of battle — VICTORIOUS.

— VINCE LOMBARDI

*The fight will be well worth the spoils
from the battle.*

— JE

The will to win is not nearly as important
as the will to prepare to win.

— BOBBY KNIGHT

Preparing for success is the key to victory!

—JE

People who suffer from a lack of
motivation suffer from a lack of
appreciation.

— ANON

*Staying motivated is difficult
if you don't take the time to find out
how good God is.*

—JE

Where the willingness is great, the
difficulties cannot be great.

— NICCOLO MACHIAVELLI

*If you execute your plan well then the problems
that you will face along the way will be like
water off a duck's back.*

—JE

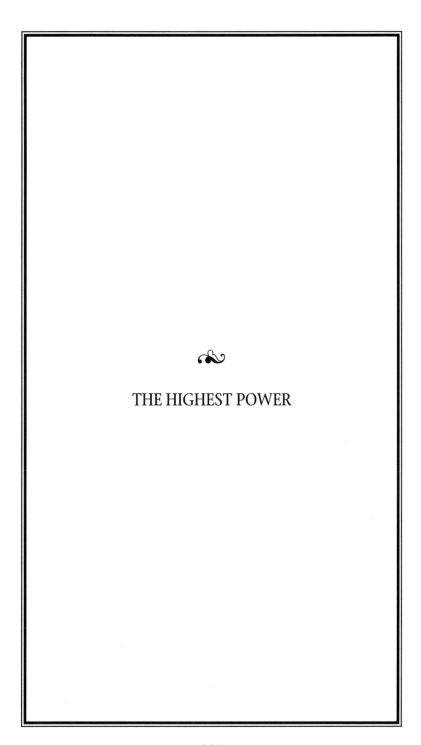

THE HIGHEST POWER

And Jesus came and spake unto them saying, "All Power is given unto me in earth and in Heaven."

— THE SON OF GOD

God is your answer, not your problem.

— JE

The power of God is what keeps me going.

— LL Cool J

You were born with the nature of God, so use it to your advantage.

— JE

God is a verb, not a noun.

— R. Buckminister Fuller

God is POWER and POWERFUL.

—JE

The most beautiful of all emblems is that
of God, whom Timaeus of Locris describes
under the image of "a circle whose center
is everywhere and whose circumference is
nowhere."

— VOLTAIRE

*HE is everywhere that you go,
so don't be afraid.*

—JE

All who call on God in true faith, earnestly
from the heart, will certainly be heard, and
will receive what they have asked and
desired.

— MARTIN LUTHER

*If you trust God with all of your heart and
pray for his blessings,
he will pour them down on you.*

—JE

Trust in the Lord with all thine heart,
and lean not unto thine own understand-
ing. In all thy ways acknowledge Him, and
He shall direct thy paths.

— Proverbs 3:5-6

*God is good all the time and He is the creator
of direction so trust in Him as you travel the
road of success.*

—JE

God is no enemy to you. He asks no more
than that He hear you call Him "Friend."

— A COURSE IN MIRACLES

*Prayer is a wonderful and powerful tool to use
everyday of your life.*

— JE

The deep emotional conviction of the presence of a superior reasoning power, which is revealed in the incomprehensible universe, forms my idea of God.

— ALBERT EINSTEIN

God is all around and the very thought of His goodness is too much for man to comprehend.

—JE

I will seek the face of God to unlock the
mysteries of this world
until I get an answer.

— GEORGE WASHINGTON CARVER

The more time that you spend with God,
the easier it is for Him to answer you.

—*JE*

When a man takes one step toward God,
God takes more steps toward that man
than there are sands in the worlds of time.

— THE WORK OF THE CHARIOT

*God wants nothing more for you to be
successful, prosperous and filled with love.*

—JE